Pianoworks
A Night at the Theatre

compiled and arranged by
Janet and Alan Bullard

MUSIC DEPARTMENT

OXFORD
UNIVERSITY PRESS

OXFORD
UNIVERSITY PRESS

Great Clarendon Street, Oxford OX2 6DP, England

Oxford University Press is a department of the University of Oxford.
It furthers the University's aim of excellence in research, scholarship,
and education by publishing worldwide

Oxford is a registered trademark of Oxford University Press
in the UK and in certain other countries

9 10 8

ISBN 978–0–19–336589–6

Music and text origination by
Barnes Music Engraving Ltd., East Sussex.
Printed in Great Britain on acid-free paper by
Halstan & Co. Ltd., Amersham, Bucks.

Contents

All pieces are arrangements by Janet and Alan Bullard.

One fine day (Un bel dì vedremo)
from *Madam Butterfly* (1904)

Giacomo Puccini
(1858–1924)

Puccini combines something of an Oriental flavour with a characteristically Italianate lyricism in this poignant aria, sung by Madam Butterfly as, full of hope, she waits for the fateful return of her errant husband Pinkerton.

Dance of the Hours
from *La Gioconda* (1880)

Amilcare Ponchielli
(1834–86)

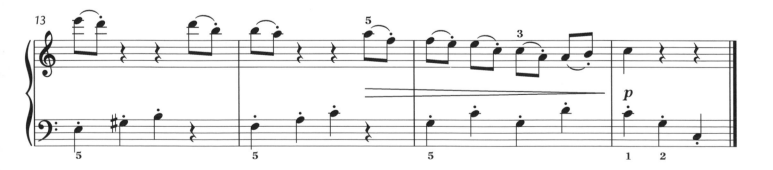

The setting for this dance scene from *La Gioconda* ('The Joyful Girl') is Alvise's palace, 'The Palace of Gold'. Unknown to the members of the nobility enjoying the delicate charm of this ballet entertainment, a complex drama is unfolding backstage involving phials of poison and bloody daggers. In recent years 'Dance of the Hours' has twice been humorously recreated—by Walt Disney in *Fantasia*, where it is danced by hippopotami and ostriches; and by Allan Sherman as the song 'Hello Muddah, Hello Faddah'.

Fairest Isle
from *King Arthur* (1691)

Henry Purcell
(1659–95)

Purcell's *King Arthur* was a typical entertainment of its time, combining spoken sections, music and dance, and spectacular dramatic effects, though it is usually performed in drastically cut concert versions today. 'Fairest Isle' is sung by the goddess Venus and forms part of a section in which the 'praises of Britain's natural resources' are sung, while Britannia benignly smiles at the fishermen at her feet.

The melody is first presented as an instrumental dance, as suggested here by the articulation.

Where is love?
from *Oliver!* (1960)

Lionel Bart
(1930–99)

Slowly and expressively

Oliver!, one of the most enduring of English musicals, was adapted from Dickens' novel *Oliver Twist*. This heart-warming song is sung by the lonely and unloved orphan boy Oliver as he tries to settle into his sleeping accommodation among the coffins of his new employer, the local undertaker. Aim to communicate the expressive qualities of the music by bringing out the flowing melodic lines in both hands with *legato* playing.

Can love be controlled by advice?

from *The Beggar's Opera* (1728)

anon.

The Beggar's Opera was a satirical tale of 'low life' by the impresario John Gay and the composer J. C. Pepusch. The duo created the opera by putting new words to popular tunes of the time, including folksongs, and arias by Handel and Purcell. It was an instant success and it partly contributed to the later demise of the wordy Italian operas of Handel which were all the rage at that time. In this aria, based on a folksong, the heroine Polly, who is married to the villain Macheath, sings that her mother's advice contradicts that of Cupid.

Barcarolle
from *The Tales of Hoffmann* (1881)

Jacques Offenbach
(1819–80)

This cameo from Offenbach's opera has captured the imagination ever since its first performance in Paris soon after the composer's death. The scene is set in Venice: in a gondola on the Grand Canal, a young couple sing the duet 'Beautiful night, O night of love' while, gathered on the ornate balcony of the palace above, the elegantly dressed guests echo the melody in the background.

Sunrise, sunset

from *Fiddler on the Roof* (1964)

Jerry Bock
(b. 1928)

'Sunrise, sunset' is sung at a wedding ceremony in this tale of a Jewish community in pre-revolutionary Russia. The guests sing of the inevitable round of day and night, life and death, happiness and tears, and how the children of yesterday are the bride and groom of today.

L'Automne
from *Ballet des saisons* (1661)

Jean-Baptiste Lully
(1632–87)

Allegretto ritmico

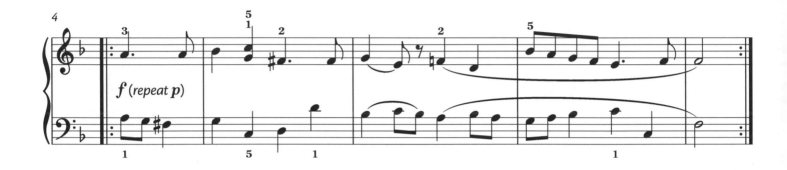

French composer Lully spent much of his life as court composer and violinist to King Louis XIV. The *Ballet des saisons* ('Ballet of the seasons') was one of thirty ballets written for the court, and in this movement the dancers took the roles of eight grape-harvesters, four female and four male.

Willow, tit-willow
from *The Mikado* (1885)

Arthur Sullivan
(1842–1900)

This song, telling of an unlikely suicide in which a small bird, crossed in love, plunges into 'the billowy wave', presents a good opportunity for the comic pathos at which Gilbert and Sullivan excelled.

Allegro un peu louré
from *Giselle* (1841)

Adolphe Adam
(1803–56)

The role of Giselle is one of the most sought after by ballet dancers. First performed in Paris, *Giselle* later became a staple of the Russian ballet repertoire. This dance, '*Allegro* in a rustic style', is sometimes known as the 'Peasant Pas de deux', typified by the repeated pedal notes in the opening section, and it was allegedly inserted into the ballet the night before the premiere in order to create a role for the mistress of one of the sponsors of the production! Despite the title, it is normally played quite steadily, but with the final section at a faster tempo, as indicated by the markings in brackets in the score. The repeats are optional.

I could be happy with you

from *The Boy Friend* (1953)

Sandy Wilson
(b. 1924)

Sandy Wilson's nostalgic take on the American musical of the 1920s was an overnight success. At Madame Dubonnet's School for Young Ladies in Nice, millionaire heiress Polly disguises herself as a secretary and falls in love with errand boy Tony. They declare their love in this duet, and plan a life of poverty and simplicity. However, Tony turns out to be a wealthy member of the aristocracy as well, so their future happiness is assured!

Moresca
from *Orfeo* (1607)

Claudio Monteverdi
(1567–1643)

Orfeo is the earliest opera still to be part of today's repertoire, and it presents a vivid spectacle, with complex staging and effects, colourful orchestration, dancing, and singing. The 'Moresca', literally 'Moorish Dance', was an exotic dance which travelled all over Europe (it's the origin of the English Morris Dance), and Monteverdi's version forms the happy finale of *Orfeo*, when Orpheus and Eurydice are reunited (see also *Che farò senza Euridice*, pp. 20–1). The music consists of the same phrase repeated four times in different keys—a beautiful example of masterly simplicity.

The Bird-catcher's Song
from *The Magic Flute* (1791)

Wolfgang Amadeus Mozart
(1756–91)

This is the first appearance in this opera of Papageno, the bird-catcher. He appears on stage with a birdcage containing a number of birds on his back, and he sings this cheerful aria, periodically interrupting the song with a blast from his panpipes, while the perplexed Tamino watches him from behind a tree.

Mack the Knife
from *The Threepenny Opera* (1928)

Kurt Weill
(1900–50)

Kurt Weill and Bertold Brecht's *Die Dreigroschenoper* ('The Threepenny Opera') is a twentieth-century adaptation of *The Beggar's Opera* (see p. 8), treating issues of injustice and corruption, and set in Victorian London. This song is sung by Mack the Knife (the same character as Macheath in *The Beggar's Opera*), and in it he compares his ability with the knife to that of the teeth of a shark, boasting of his skill as a murderer.

Che farò senza Euridice
from *Orfeo ed Euridice* (1762)

C. W. Gluck
(1714–87)

Many composers have been attracted by the universality of the Greek myth of Orpheus and Eurydice. Here, Orpheus has been given dispensation by the gods to visit his dead lover Eurydice and to bring her back with him, but he is forbidden to look at her until she is safely home. Unfortunately Eurydice does not realize this, so when she insists that Orpheus turns to see her, she returns to the kingdom of the dead. Orpheus then sings this song, asking himself 'What shall I do without Eurydice?'. Moved by his singing, the God of Love rewards Orpheus for his constancy, and brings Eurydice back to life.

Dances
from *The Little Shepherd* (13th cent.)

anon.
Chinese opera

This piece is based on fragments of two dances from *The Little Shepherd*, an opera dating from the thirteenth century. The traditions of Chinese opera have continued relatively unchanged over the past millennium and it has shown a capacity for reinventing itself during the dances various dynasties and political changes of China's history. Today Peking (Beijing) Opera is a popular spectacle in theatres and on television, and dances such as these are still performed.

Ombra mai fù
from *Xerxes (Serse)* (1738)

George Frideric Handel
(1685–1759)

Xerxes was first performed at the Haymarket Theatre in London, but apart from this movement it was not a success: it received just five performances, and was not performed again until a German revival in 1924, nearly 200 years later. This aria ('So beautiful a shade'), which is probably better known in the instrumental version, Handel's *Largo*, is sung by Xerxes, who tells of the beauty of a plane tree in his garden.

On the street where you live
from *My Fair Lady* (1956)

Frederick Loewe
(1901–88)

One of the most popular of all musicals, Lerner and Loewe's *My Fair Lady* is based on George Bernard Shaw's play *Pygmalion*. In this scene Eliza, a London flower-girl, is inside the grand Wimpole Street house of her elocution teacher, Professor Henry Higgins, who has plans to make her a lady of quality. Meanwhile, her suitor Freddy paces up and down the street outside singing of his love for her.

The Flight of the Swans
from *Swan Lake* (1877)

Pyotr Il'yich Tchaikovsky
(1840–93)

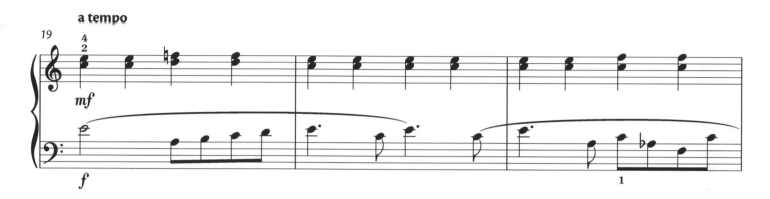

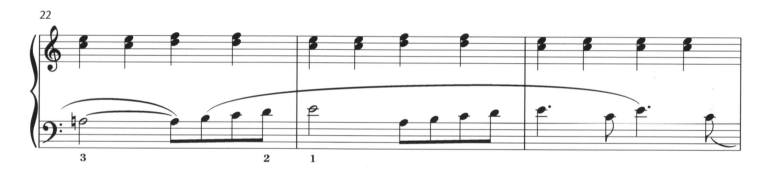

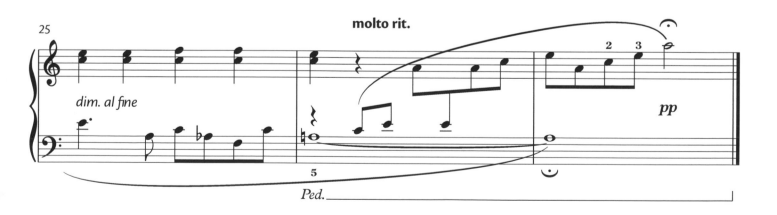

It perhaps rather spoils this calm and peaceful picture of the swans gently flying through the evening sky to know that in Tchaikovsky's ballet they are actually being hunted with cross-bows by the Prince and his companion. Despite this, the swans maintain their graceful poise, which provides a good opportunity in this arrangement for a singing *legato* in the left hand.

Soldiers' Chorus
from *Faust* (1859)

Charles-François Gounod
(1818–93)

Alla marcia

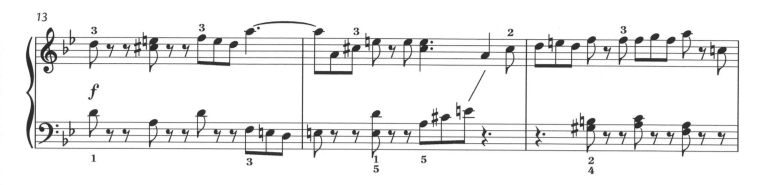

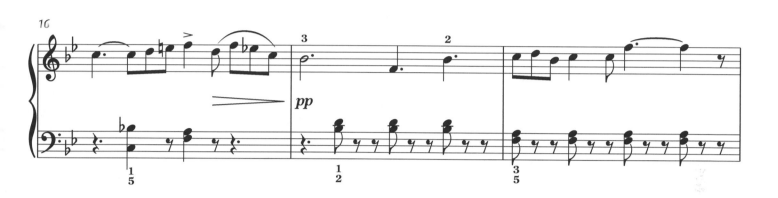

Set outside the window of the heroine Marguerite, this rousing chorus appears towards the end of the opera, where it provides dramatic relief from the unfolding tragedy caused by Faust having sold his soul to the devil (Mephistopheles) in return for the promise of eternal youth.

Waltz
from *Die Fledermaus* (1874)

Johann Strauss
(1825–99)

Strauss's light-hearted operetta *Die Fledermaus* ('The Bat') is full of memorable tunes, and this one celebrates love, champagne, and dancing in a lively waltz. Hold back bar 17 for as long as you dare—then swing back into tempo!

Don't dilly dally on the way (My old man)
British music-hall song (1918)

Fred W. Leigh (1871–1924)
and Charles Collins (1874–1923)

With robust good humour

The music-hall was a popular theatrical spectacular of Victorian and Edwardian times, and this song was popularized by Marie Lloyd, one of the most characterful entertainers of her day. It tells of a 'moonlight flit', to avoid paying the rent, in which the singer ignores the advice of her 'old man' to 'follow the van and don't dilly dally on the way', and instead stops for a drink and loses the way to her new home.

Polka
from *The Bartered Bride* (1866)

Bedřich Smetana
(1824–84)

Allegretto vivo

Based on a Bohemian folk-tale, and incorporating many dances in the folk style, Smetana's opera quickly became a national institution for the Czech people. The Polka, one of the most popular of Bohemian dances, is exuberant but not hurried, with energetic rhythms.

Toreador's Song
from *Carmen* (1875)

Georges Bizet
(1838–75)

Allegro moderato

Despite its initial poor reception, *Carmen* quickly became one of the most popular operas of the French tradition, with performances in Vienna, London, and New York running successfully within three years of Bizet's untimely death shortly after the first performance. Its tale, of a soldier whose life and career are wrecked by his love for the enchanting and seductive Carmen, provides Bizet with plenty of scope for colour and drama. This aria, sung by the toreador Escamillo—who is shortly to usurp the soldier's place in Carmen's heart—brings the colour and excitement of the bull fight to the operatic stage.

Cabaret
from *Cabaret* (1966)

John Kander (b. 1927)
and Fred Ebb (1928–2004)

Cabaret, based loosely on Isherwood's book *Goodbye to Berlin*, is set in a seedy Berlin nightclub in the early 1930s. This song recreates the 1930s style and is sung by the heroine Sally Bowles (played by Judi Dench in the first UK performances), who is trying to maintain her spirits against a background of riots, persecution, and lost love.

Largo al factotum (Figaro's Aria)

from *The Barber of Seville* (1816)

Gioachino Rossini
(1792–1868)

In this witty and boastful aria Figaro, the town barber and general busybody, accompanies himself on the guitar. He tells his audience how nothing can happen in Seville without him knowing of it, and that he can influence its outcome as well.

Ceremonial March
from *Die Meistersinger* (1868)

Richard Wagner
(1813–83)

Molto moderato e grandioso

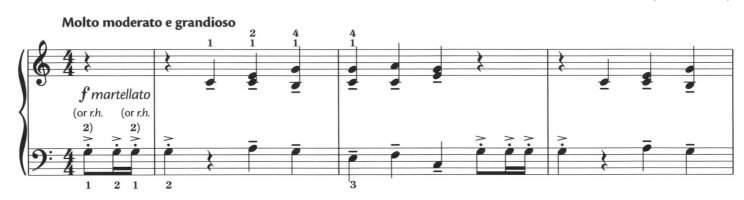

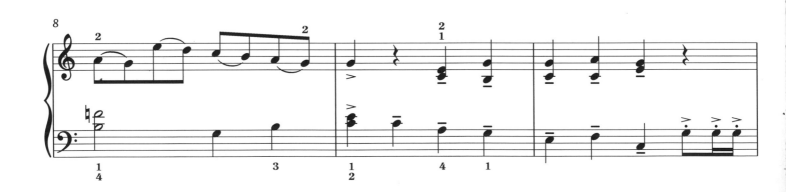

Based on a seventeenth-century melody attributed to the Nuremberg Guild of Mastersingers, this excerpt from the overture to Wagner's opera captures the mood of pomp and ceremony in anticipation of the grand singing competition to follow. The repeated left-hand Gs on the first page can also be played with the second fingers of alternating hands, as indicated.

Evening Prayer
from *Hansel and Gretel* (1893)

Engelbert Humperdinck
(1854–1921)

Humperdinck's opera about the witch who lures Hansel and Gretel to her house made of sugar and sweets contains several charming set pieces. Here, the two children, lost in the scary forest, kneel and sing their evening prayers surrounded by a vision of fourteen angels.